Praise for

THE M WORD *JOURNAL*:
HOW TO HAVE THE *MONEY TALK*

"Successful wealth management often starts with open and honest conversations about money and its role in a family's life goals. Lori Sackler's *The M Word Journal* is a practical handbook for anyone looking to have these critical Money Talks with their parents and children across a wide range of life events. With easy-to-follow worksheets and instructions, the book guides you through these important and sometimes difficult conversations to help secure your family's financial future."

—Shelley O'Connor, Co-Head of Wealth Management, Morgan Stanley

"With her insightful book *The M Word*, Lori Sackler showed us how to tackle the difficult financial decisions that families face such as when to retire and how to care for elderly parents. Now with *The M Word Journal*, she spells out the concrete steps families must follow to tackle these decisions successfully."

—Richard Marston, Professor of Finance and Director of the Private Wealth Management Program at the Wharton School

"*The M Word Journal* is an accessible easy-to-use workbook that will help address one of the most difficult of life's issues—money. The book takes readers with simple questions and templates through the most volatile of money situations: changes, remarriage, retirement, elderly parents, and inheritance. If using this workbook serves as the catalyst for even an hour-long conversation on any of these topics, both you and your loved ones will benefit handsomely."

—Martin M. Shenkman, CPA, MBA, AEP, PFS, JD, estate attorney and author

"Lori Sackler continues to dazzle and sparkle with her wise investment judgment and her experience-based insights into the complexities of family dynamics and the money conversations ensuing therefrom. *The M Word Journal* provides THE detailed roadmap for all investors and their family members to successfully navigate life's defining transitions."

—David M. Darst, CFA, Founder of, Senior Advisor to, and member of Morgan Stanley's Global Investment Committee

"How to Have the Money Talk! With insight and knowledge, Lori Sackler in *the M Word Journal* takes the reader through the steps that will lead you through the productive conversations necessary for successful financial decisions. In concert with *the M Word*, she will help reduce the financial anxiety and stress in your life and enhance your overall sense of well-being."

—Hendrie Weisinger, Ph.D., *New York Times* bestseller, *Performing Under Pressure: The Science of Doing Your Best When it Matters Most*

"This journal is very well organized with an array of practical charts for each life transition category. I especially appreciate Lori's thoughtful, positive approach in asking the many open-ended questions. A most mindful guide to having conversations about money."

—Eileen Gallo, PhD, coauthor with Jon Gallo of *Silver Spoon Kids*

The M Word Journal:
How to Have the Money Talk
by Lori R. Sackler

ISBN 978-1-63393-258-6

Morgan Stanley is held harmless with regard to any legal or other issues that may arise from the advice and examples used in this book.

Tax laws are complex and subject to change. The information in this book is based on current federal tax laws in effect at the time the book was written and should not be construed as advice on tax and tax accounting matters. Individuals should consult their own legal, tax investment, or other advisors to determine the laws and analyses applicable to their specific circumstances.

Published by

köehlerbooks™

210 60th Street
Virginia Beach, VA 23451
212-574-7939
www.koehlerbooks.com

The M Word JOURNAL

HOW TO HAVE THE MONEY TALK

LORI R. SACKLER

CONTENTS

We confess everything else in our society—sex, crime, illness.
But no one wants to reveal what they earn or how they got it.

—BARBARA EHRENREICH

INTRODUCTION

Since the 2013 publication of my first book, *The M Word: The Money Talk Every Family Needs to Have about Wealth and Their Financial Future,* I have learned that my M-Word message definitely resonates. Regardless of the level of wealth, size, cultural background, configuration, or gender composition, every family struggles with successfully handling money issues and the money talks that are essential to avoid failure. The conversations, like the financial challenges, are complicated and, for some, can be terrifying—which is why I wrote *The M Word.* It provides a five-step process to guide individuals and families through the talks and ultimately the major life events, or transition points, that make the talks necessary.

The response to my book continues to be extremely positive, affirming, and personally rewarding. Some of the most insightful feedback from readers, including the April 6, 2013 *New York Times* review, reflects a need for more substantive tools and specific guidance for family discussions. *The M Word* helps the public understand why the "Money Talk" is such a daunting task given the many conscious and unconscious factors that interfere and provides compelling arguments for having the conversations. But the book does not focus enough on the "how to" step in the process—how to actually talk to your family about money does matter. Readers need a more comprehensive road map for the conversations: hence, the reason for *The M Word Journal: How to Have the Money Talk.*

The M Word Journal will provide individuals and families a detailed outline for asking the right financial questions at each transition point, for gathering the necessary financial information, and for preparing and conducting the talks. I believe it will serve as the foundation for conversations between the parties to the discussions for both family members and their advisors. You may not be able to get through the complete questionnaire and road map because *The M Word Journal*, by design, is comprehensive. Also, you may need to refer to my first book, *The M Word*, as you make your way through this one. But having a disciplined approach embodied in this document, and sharing this document with others, may help you and your family keep your money and family relationships intact as you struggle with life's challenges. *The M Word Journal* is a vehicle to generate interest among those involved, get each other's feedback, and ultimately spark members of the family to action.

I've spent considerable time trying to include all the questions and fact-gathering elements necessary to master each of the five transition points I've identified. I hope you will feel inspired to explore issues on your own and by doing so, create your own personal, tailored approach. My goal is to help you move the process along.

Good luck with your Money Talks!

ACKNOWLEDGMENTS

As with my first publication, there are many people to thank for their work, wisdom, wealth of professional insights, and input into this project. My agent, Leah Spiro, as with *The M Word: The Money Talk Every Family Needs to Have about Wealth and their Financial Future*, was a principal contributor to *The M Word Journal's* evolution, guiding me with her special brand of publishing expertise and experience, from the original concept, to manuscript, and finally to actual print with lots of weekly phone calls and weekend reviews along the way. Mark Levine, my editor for *The M Word,* played a critical role in the development of the content, and I will always be grateful for his logical and very thoughtful approach. Special thanks also goes to Tom Lau, the art director on the project, for his creative input and interactive touch on the final presentation.

The professionals at McGraw-Hill—Donya Dickerson, Christopher Brown, and Yin Chan were critically important to the release of the second edition of *The M Word: The Money Talk*, for which I am very grateful. And I am especially appreciative of the professionals at Koehler Books–John Koehler, Joe Coccaro, and Cheryl Ross, who worked diligently to realize my goal and dream of bringing *The M Word Journal* to the public.

I am particularly grateful to the wonderful people at Morgan Stanley who spent considerable professional time and energy at various stages of the project so that I could give birth to ANOTHER manuscript. My sincerest gratitude to my best-ever branch management team: Rich Less, Ardell Roan, Kathe Koch, George Batelli, Ed Wilson, Bo Skala, and the best-in-class legal, compliance, and wealth management team at Morgan Stanley: Rick Apicella, Glenn Kurlander, Vincent Lumia, Les Klein, and Paul Stam.

The marketing professionals at Morgan Stanley: Jim Wiggins, Margaret Draper, and Christine Jockle have been extremely supportive of my M-Word message over the years in a variety of impactful ways, including connecting me with Michael London and his colleague Debbie Levinson, both consummate public relations professionals with whom I have enjoyed working. And my publicist and public relations partner, Meryl Moss, and her staff have been essential in my efforts to get *The M Word: The Money Talk* into the public domain and are now spreading the word about *The M Word Journal: How to Have the Money Talk.*

Special thanks to the members of my Morgan Stanley team, the Sackler Group at Morgan Stanley: Henry Sackler, my partner, who by his hard work and enormous contributions to the practice has helped free up my weekends and evenings to give me time to devote to the project; and my assistants, Nancy Hecker and Chantana Suwansiri, who make a difference in their daily commitment to our mission of caring for our clients and their families.

My dear family, husband Michael, and sons Eliot and Henry, are the essentials in my life and part of the reason I'm motivated to give back in a more public way through *The M Word* and my community volunteer projects.

And, finally, thanks to the Sackler Group clients who have played an enormous role in the evolving M-Word concept. They continue to challenge our thinking and approach to wealth management while giving us a sense of pride and joy in the work that we do for them each day.

CHANGES IN FINANCIAL CIRCUMSTANCES

Having Money Talks When Disaster Strikes or When Good Fortune Comes Your Way

I'm living so far beyond my income that we may almost be said to be living apart.

—E.E. CUMMINGS

Our financial circumstances undergo significant changes over the course of our lifetimes, and our family members' financial situations change as well. Whether it's a death, a work promotion, or a business reversal, change is a fact of life and these changes can be either positive or negative. If we don't adapt to the new situations, align income and expenses, and get the participants on board, the repercussions could be serious. Under normal circumstances, the subject of money is difficult for families to discuss. When there have been significant changes in financial circumstances, the natural human tendency is for everyone to shut down emotionally and avoid the conversation.

But not discussing these life changes can be costly—and not just in dollars and cents. Existing issues and family conflicts are likely to be exacerbated, and new ones are apt to emerge along with the ramifications of changed financial circumstances. Acknowledgment, disclosure, and discussion are the keys to emerging from these changes with family finances and dynamics intact.

Note: Before you address the specific issue you are facing, make sure you have updated your personal financial inventory and records. You will need access to the most up-to-date information in order to complete this *M Word Journal*, which is designed around the following five steps:

1. Gather information about the transition point you are facing, and identify and prepare for the issues and topics that need to be discussed.
2. Consider the factors that are interfering with you and your family having the Money Talk and how to overcome them.
3. Plan the Money Talk physically, logistically, and psychologically.
4. Determine what professional help you may need for the Money Talk.
5. Create a process, repeat it, and anticipate and plan for future Money Talks.

PLEASE NOTE: For an in-depth explanation of the Money Talk and other concepts in this Journal, see *The M Word: The Money Talk Every Family Needs to Have about Wealth and Their Financial Future* (McGraw-Hill Education, 2013, updated 2016).

STEP 1: Gather information about the transition point you are facing, and identify and prepare for the issues and topics that need to be discussed.

1.1: Review your assets.

ASSET	ESTIMATED AMOUNT
Bank accounts	
Brokerage accounts	
Securities	
IRAs/Profit sharing/401(k) plans	
Stock options/Restricted stock/Deferred compensation	
Pensions/Annuities	
Insurance (cash value)	
Real estate	
Autos	
Home furnishings	
Collectibles	
Other/Business interests/etc.	
Total	

1.2: Review your liabilities.

LIABILITY	AMOUNT
Mortgage balances	
Auto loans	
Student loans	
Personal loans	
Personal lines of credit	
Credit card balances	
Personally guaranteed business loans	
Other itemized debts	
Total	

1.3: Review your family's current income stream.

EARNED INCOME	MONTHLY	ANNUALLY
Spouse/Partner 1		
Spouse/Partner 2		
Total		

INCOME FROM INVESTMENTS/SECURITIES	MONTHLY	ANNUALLY
Spouse/Partner 1		
Spouse/Partner 2		
Total		

INCOME FROM BUSINESS INTERESTS AND REAL ESTATE	MONTHLY	ANNUALLY
Spouse/Partner 1		
Spouse/Partner 2		
Total		

INCOME FROM SOCIAL SECURITY, ANNUITIES, PENSIONS, IRAS, 401(K)S, ETC., IF AVAILABLE	MONTHLY	ANNUALLY
Spouse/Partner 1		
Spouse/Partner 2		
Total		

INCOME FROM OTHER SOURCES[1]	MONTHLY	ANNUALLY
Spouse 1		
Spouse 2		
Total		

WHAT IS YOUR TOTAL INCOME?	MONTHLY	ANNUALLY
Earned income		
Investments/securities		
Business interests/real estate		
Social Security and retirement assets		
Other Sources		
Total		

1.4: Review your family's current expenses and obligations.

EXPENSE	MONTHLY	ANNUALLY
Primary home[2]		
Secondary home[3]		
Food		
Clothing		

[1] Sources might include annual gifts, trust income, part-time work, real estate income, etc.

[2] Include all expenses involved in maintenance of the property as well as taxes and mortgage or rent payments.

1.4: Review your family's current expenses and obligations (continued).

EXPENSE	MONTHLY	ANNUALLY
Personal entertainment		
Utilities[4]		
Personal transportation[5]		
Other debt service[6]		
Taxes		
Professional fees		
Travel		
Dues and memberships		
Insurance[7]		
Education[8]		
Child support		
Alimony		
Pension contribution		
Regular savings		
Total		

EXPENSES RELATED TO NON-DEPENDENT CHILDREN AND PARENTS[9]	MONTHLY	ANNUALLY
Total		

[3] Include all expenses involved in the maintenance of the property as well as taxes and mortgage or rent payments.

[4] Include cell phone, pay television, and Internet services.

[5] Include mass transit and auto expenses like gas, parking, maintenance, insurance, and lease or loan payments.

[6] Include other liabilities, such as lines of credit, credit card debt, and other real estate loans not included above.

[7] Include medical as well as life, disability, homeowners, and umbrella/liability policies.

[8] Include tuition, room and board, books, and other education-related items.

[9] Itemize expenses.

1.5: Calculate the current surplus or shortfall.

	MONTHLY	ANNUALLY
Total income		
Total expenses and obligations		
Surplus or shortfall		

1.6: If there is a shortfall, can you restructure or pay off any of your debts?

DEBT	MONTHLY SAVINGS	ANNUAL SAVINGS
Total		

1.7: If there is a shortfall, can you trim any of your living expenses and obligations?

EXPENSE	MONTHLY SAVINGS	ANNUAL SAVINGS
Total		

1.8: If there is a shortfall, can your family develop any new streams of income, such as a nonworking spouse going to work, a family member who is working part time going full time, or a dependent child getting part-time employment?

ADDITIONAL STREAM OF INCOME	MONTHLY INCREASE	ANNUAL INCREASE
Total		

1.9: If there is a shortfall, consider reductions in contributions to adult non-dependent children, parents, and charitable donations.

CONTRIBUTION	MONTHLY SAVINGS	ANNUAL SAVINGS
Total		

1.10: If there is a shortfall, consult with your financial advisor regarding other possible changes to cope with reduced circumstances such as the sale of real estate, a business interest, securities, or personal property (art, collectibles, etc.).

POSSIBLE CHANGE	MONTHLY SAVINGS	ANNUAL SAVINGS
Total		

1.11: If there is a surplus, consult with your financial advisor and update your financial and estate plans to reflect the "new normal." Consider expanding your investment portfolio, investing in an existing or new business, purchasing a second home, incorporating selective lending opportunities, and increasing gifts and charitable giving.

STEP 2: Consider the factors that are interfering with your family having the Money Talk and how to overcome them.

2.1: How has money been used as a means of control in your immediate family? How has that affected the various relationships, and how does it continue to inform them?

____

____

____

2.2: In what ways are money and trust bound together in your immediate family culture? How does that play out in family relationships, collectively and individually?

2.3: What is the historical role of each member of the immediate family when it comes to money? Has someone been the caretaker, while someone else has always needed to be cared for? Has a member of the family always been responsible and independent, while another member has always been irresponsible and more dependent? How will changes in the family and money structure affect these roles?

2.4: Accept that gender differences have roots in physiology and as a result, anticipate some conflicts. Which differences will be at work in your situation: risk-taking, prioritizing of goals, setting a time horizon, or all three?

2.5: Be aware of the ingrained thinking patterns that influence decisions. What are the issues in this situation that could lead to a struggle between emotion and reason when it comes to making money decisions? For example, . . .

2.6: Understand that people are hardwired to see money as an object of threat and control, causing them to respond instinctively. Which of the six basic instincts—shelter seeking, care soliciting, caregiving, cooperation, beauty, and curiosity—are likely to arise in each of the participants, and what are the best ways to address them? (Refer to chapter 8 of *The M Word*.)

2.7: Understand generational differences in money perceptions and values. What generational differences will you face in this situation? What language can you use that is age- and generation-appropriate?

2.8: Think about your extended family's history with money. Has the relationship that parents and grandparents had with money been passed down to any of the other participants in the Money Talk? For example, historically, has money been used as a substitute for love or a tool for control or for some other tactic? How might this history play out in the current situation, and how can you address it?

2.9: Understand that culture and experience affect attitudes about money. Are there any cultural or regional differences in attitudes that you will face in this Money Talk? Is the immigrant experience "fresher" for some participants of the Money Talk than others?

2.10: Couple politics can also impact Money Talks, particularly when one partner surpasses the other in education and/or earning power. Are there any such issues that you will face in this Money Talk?

STEP 3: Plan the Money Talk physically, logistically, and psychologically.

3.1: Have you ever held a Money Talk before? If so, what happened?

3.2: What do you think made earlier Money Talks successes or failures?

3.3: What are your concerns, if any, about holding this particular Money Talk?

3.4: What are your objectives or goals for this Money Talk? What do you want to accomplish?

3.5: What are the specific financial issues and topics you'll need to address that were identified in Step 1?

3.6: Are there any potentially problematic family issues that are likely to arise? Are there factors related to control, trust, family health, gender, marriage politics, evolutionary patterns, instinctive behavior, family history, culture, age, attitude, etc.? (This topic is covered in Chapters 8 and 11 in *The M Word*.)

3.7: Is there anyone in the family with whom communicating is frequently challenging? If so, who?

3.8: Is there anything you can do to overcome these factors and individual challenges?

3.9: Using professional communication techniques (discussed in Chapter 9 in *The M Word*), answer who, what, when, where, and how to have the talk before sitting down for the conversations. Create an agenda based on the issues at play and the players that need to be present. Chapter 3 in *The M Word* includes a sample agenda and more discussion around creating an agenda tailored to your talk.

____

____

____

3.10: Well in advance of the Money Talk, send a summary agenda to everyone who will be party to the conversation so they can be prepared to discuss the topics and, if appropriate, address them in advance with their advisor(s). Speak to each participant before the meeting regarding the meeting objectives and their particular concerns, and make any necessary changes to the agenda to reflect additional issues raised. Inform participants that communication devices are not permitted during the talks. Make sure you have agendas printed and available at the Money Talk.

3.11: Based on the agenda, write a "script" for exactly what you want to say and how you want to say it, and then rehearse it.

____

____

____

3.12: Consider times and settings for the talk that can create a safe and comfortable environment. (Refer to Chapter 8 in *The M Word*.)

____

____

____

3.13: To enhance the chances for success, apologize for any role you may have played in creating family conflict. Develop appropriate language and tone to help facilitate caring and cooperation.

3.14: Plan a question-and-answer session and your responses to anticipated concerns and expressions of anger or resentment using inquiry, acknowledgment, advocacy, and problem solving techniques. (Refer to Chapter 9 in *The M Word.*)

3.15: Plan to discuss changes you will need to make to your current lifestyle that could impact other family members.

3.16: Plan to discuss changes to your long-term financial planning that could impact other family members.

STEP 4: Determine what professional help you may need for the Money Talk.

4.1: Do you have an advisor(s) who can help you with your collective and individual tax, estate, and financial planning?

- ☐ Yes
- ☐ No

4.2 If you have an advisor(s), have you discussed with them your ideal outcome for the talk and the financial issues and topics that may need to be discussed? If you do not have advisors, what professionals do you think you need in order to create the right team?

- ☐ Accountant
- ☐ Attorney
- ☐ Financial advisor
- ☐ Mental health professional
- ☐ Other

4.3: If you do have a team and you want to replace one or more members, who are they? Why are you not satisfied with them? What traits would you look for in replacement members that the current members of your team lack?

____

____

____

4.4: Does your advisor(s) have the right combination of licenses, credentials, experience, and knowledge in the areas you need?

☐ Yes

☐ No

4.5: Do they have the necessary character and chemistry as well as the communication skills you are looking for?

☐ Yes

☐ No

4.6: Are you prepared to do all the work that needs to be done to find the right advisor or team of advisors?

☐ Yes

☐ No

4.7: If you are not prepared to conduct the search, is there another member of your family who can do it? Is there a member of your professional team who can refer you to qualified professionals and may be capable of doing the initial search for you?

____

____

____

4.8: What situations are facing your family that you need to address when you interview advisor candidates?

____

____

____

4.9: Is there anything unique about your family that should be discussed with potential advisors? Is there a special expertise you might need in order to deal with current or future issues?

4.10: Do any of your existing advisors appear to have the ability to act as team quarterback? If not, do any of the advisors you are interviewing appear to have the ability to act as quarterback?

4.11: Is there a professional advisor or trusted third party who can help you prepare for the Money Talk or perhaps even lead it?

STEP 5: Anticipate and plan for future Money Talks.

5.1: Was the Money Talk a success? If so, why? If not, why?

5.2: Have you created a process that is repeatable, and have you planned for the multiple conversations that are probably necessary for accomplishing your goals?

____

____

____

5.3: What issues related to this transition, either newly developed or raised in the most recent Money Talk, will you need to discuss or review in the near future?

____

____

____

5.4: What is the best method for regular periodic money discussions if in-person discussions are not available for everyone for future talks?

- ☐ Telephone calls
- ☐ Skype/FaceTime
- ☐ Email/Text—for transmitting information only
- ☐ Other

5.5: When and where will you hold your next Money Talk? Who will prepare the next agenda and take the leadership role in planning?

____

____

____

ANNUIT COEPTIS
2

REMARRIAGE AND MERGING FAMILIES

HAVING MONEY TALKS WHEN DIVORCING AND/OR GETTING MARRIED AGAIN

A divorce is like an amputation: you survive it, but there's less of you.

—Margaret Atwood

ANNUIT COEPTIS

It's an unfortunate fact that half of all first marriages end in divorce. Second and third marriages, which often involve the merging of families, have an even greater chance of not surviving.

Whether a remarriage is successful in the long term or not, the blending of families is difficult and may be a factor in whether the marriage succeeds. Despite bringing wisdom to the new marriage that has been hard-earned from past mistakes, individuals are more set in their ways. In addition, individuals may have children, all of whom have unique and potentially conflicting characteristics. It's a challenging task to combine the new family dynamics with possibly incompatible work and activity schedules as well as separate financial assets and obligations, plus disparate goals and values. Add to that the need to work through the emotional issues of loss and oftentimes anger stemming from divorce or death that precedes the new combination, and the task becomes even more daunting.

There is one thing that can make this transition smoother: Both partners must disclose not just their financial circumstances and contributions to children and parents, but also their psyches surrounding money, money philosophies, and family histories. Financial adjustments and compromises are often easier to accomplish than shifts in family culture.

Note: Before you address the specific issue you are facing, make sure you have updated your personal financial inventory and records. You will need access to the most up-to-date information in order to complete this *M Word Journal*, which is designed around the following five steps:

1. Gather information about the transition point you are facing, and identify and prepare for the issues and topics that need to be discussed.
2. Consider the factors that are interfering with your family having the Money Talk and how to overcome them.
3. Plan the Money Talk physically, logistically, and psychologically.
4. Determine what professional help you may need for the Money Talk.
5. Create a process, repeat it, and anticipate and plan for future Money Talks.

PLEASE NOTE: For an in-depth discussion of the Money Talk and other concepts in this chapter, see *The M Word: The Money Talk Every Family Needs to Have about Wealth and Their Financial Future* (McGraw-Hill Education, 2013, updated 2016).

STEP 1: Gather information about the transition point you are facing, and identify and prepare for the issues and topics that need to be discussed.

1.1: Review your assets.

ASSET	ESTIMATED AMOUNT
Bank accounts	
Brokerage accounts	
Securities	
IRAs/Profit sharing/401(k) plans	
Stock options/Restricted stock/Deferred compensation	
Pensions/Annuities	
Insurance (cash value)	
Real estate	
Autos	
Home furnishings	
Collectibles	
Other/Business interests/etc.	
Total	

1.2: Review your liabilities.

LIABILITY	SPOUSE/PARTNER 1	SPOUSE/PARTNER 2
Mortgage balances		
Auto loans		
Student loans		
Personal loans		
Personal lines of credit		
Credit card balances		
Personally guaranteed business loans		
Other itemized debts		
Total		

1.3: Review your individual and combined income streams.

EARNED INCOME	MONTHLY	ANNUALLY
Spouse/Partner 1		
Spouse/Partner 2		
Total		

INCOME FROM INVESTMENTS/SECURITIES	MONTHLY	ANNUALLY
Spouse/Partner 1		
Spouse/Partner 2		
Total		

INCOME FROM BUSINESS INTERESTS/REAL ESTATE	MONTHLY	ANNUALLY
Spouse/Partner 1		
Spouse/Partner 2		
Total		

INCOME FROM RETIREMENT ASSETS: SOCIAL SECURITY, ANNUITIES, PENSIONS, IRAS, 401(K)S, ETC., IF AVAILABLE	MONTHLY	ANNUALLY
Spouse/Partner 1		
Spouse/Partner 2		
Total		

INCOME FROM OTHER SOURCES[1]	MONTHLY	ANNUALLY
Spouse 1		
Spouse 2		
Total		

WHAT IS YOUR TOTAL INCOME?	MONTHLY	ANNUALLY
Earned income		
Investments/securities		
Business interests/real estate		
Social Security and retirement assets		
Other sources		
Total		

[1] Sources might include annual gifts, trust income, part-time work, alimony/child support, etc.

1.4: Review your family's current expenses and obligations.

EXPENSE	SPOUSE/PARTNER 1	SPOUSE/PARTNER 2
Primary home[2]		
Secondary home[3]		
Food		
Clothing		
Personal entertainment		
Utilities[4]		
Personal transportation[5]		
Other debt service[6]		
Taxes		
Professional fees		
Travel		
Dues and memberships		
Insurance[7]		
Education[8]		
Child support		
Alimony		
Pension contribution		
Regular savings		
Total		

[2] Include all expenses involved in the upkeep and maintenance of the property as well as any mortgage or rent payments.

[3] Include all expenses involved in the upkeep and maintenance of the property as well as any mortgage or rent payments.

[4] Include cell phone, pay television, and Internet services.

[5] Include any mass transit/commuting costs as well as auto lease or loan payments, auto insurance, fuel, repairs, and maintenance.

[6] Do NOT include home mortgages or children's student loans.

[7] Include medical as well as life, disability, homeowners, and umbrella/liability policies.

[8] Include tuition, room and board, books, and other education-related items.

EXPENSES RELATED TO NON-DEPENDENT CHILDREN AND PARENTS[9]	SPOUSE/PARTNER 1	SPOUSE/PARTNER 2
Total		

1.5: Consider the division of future merged expenses.

EXPENSE	TOTAL	SPOUSE/ PARTNER 1	SPOUSE/ PARTNER 2
Primary home			
Secondary home			
Food			
Clothing			
Personal entertainment			
Utilities			
Personal transportation			
Other debt service			
Taxes			
Professional fees			
Travel			
Dues and memberships			
Insurance			
Other expenses			

[9] Itemize expenses.

1.6: What are your goals and aspirations for your money?

Spouse/Partner 1: ______________________________

____

Spouse/Partner 2:: ______________________________

____

1.7: What does money mean to you? What are your money values?

Spouse/Partner 1: ______________________________

____

Spouse/Partner 2:: ______________________________

____

1.8: What has been your family history and culture around money?

Spouse/Partner 1: ______________________________

____

Spouse/Partner 2:: ______________________________

____

1.9: How would you describe your philosophy about providing financially for your dependent children? Do you give priority to providing as much help as you can, or do you find ways to encourage their financial independence?

Spouse/Partner 1: ______________________________

____

Spouse/Partner 2:: ______________________________

____

1.10: How would you describe your philosophy about providing financially for your adult children and elderly parents? Would you give priority to providing as much help to them as you can or to maintaining your own lifestyle?

Spouse/Partner 1: ______________________________

____

Spouse/Partner 2:: ______________________________

____

1.11: How would you describe your investment philosophy? Are you more concerned with security/safety or with your investment return?

Spouse/Partner 1: ______________________________

____

Spouse/Partner 2:: ______________________________

____

1.12: How do you feel about losing money? Are you more interested in short-term gains or in holding investments long term?

Spouse/Partner 1: ______________________________

____

Spouse/Partner 2:: ______________________________

____

1.13: Are your investment goals more about caring for the children and grandchildren or your personal goals, such as retirement?

Spouse/Partner 1: ______________________________

____

Spouse/Partner 2:: ______________________________

____

1.14: How do you feel about working with advisors, and how do you feel about your current advisors? Do you need to make changes?

Spouse/Partner 1: ______________________________

____

Spouse/Partner 2:: ______________________________

____

1.15: Can you describe your current financial and estate plans? How would you describe your estate or legacy philosophy? Are you more concerned with providing for your heirs after your death or with preparing them and transferring assets to them while you're alive?

Spouse/Partner 1: ______________________________

____

Spouse/Partner 2:: ______________________________

____

1.16: What are your charitable goals?

Spouse/Partner 1: ______________________________

____

Spouse/Partner 2:: ______________________________

____

STEP 2: Consider the factors that are interfering with your family having the Money Talk and how to overcome them.

2.1: How has money been used as a means of control in your immediate family? How has that affected the various relationships, and how does it continue to inform them?

2.2: In what ways are money and trust bound together in your immediate family culture? How does that play out in family relationships, collectively and individually?

2.3: What is the historical role of each member of the immediate family when it comes to money? Has someone been the caretaker while someone else always needed to be cared for? Has a member of the family always been responsible and independent, whereas another member has always been irresponsible and more dependent? And how will changes in the family and money structure affect these roles?

2.4: Accept that gender differences have roots in physiology and as a result, some conflicts are likely. Which differences will be at work in your situation: risk-taking, prioritizing of goals, setting a time horizon, or all three?

____

____

____

2.5: Be aware of the ingrained thinking patterns that influence decisions. What are the issues in this situation that could lead to a struggle between emotion and reason when it comes to making money decisions? For example, . . .

____

____

____

2.6: Understand that people are hardwired to see money as an object of threat and control and often respond instinctively. Which of the six basic instincts—shelter seeking, care soliciting, caregiving, cooperation, beauty, and curiosity—are likely to arise in each of the participants and what are the best ways to address them? (Refer to Chapter 8 of *The M Word*.)

____

____

____

2.7: Understand generational differences in money perceptions and values. What generational differences will you face in this situation? What language can you use that's age- and generation-appropriate?

____

____

____

2.8: Think about your extended family's history with money. Has the relationship that parents and grandparents had with money been passed down to any of the other participants in the Money Talk? For example, historically, has money been used as a substitute for love or a tool for control or for some other tactic? How might this history play out in the current situation and how might you address it?

2.9: Understand that culture and experience affect attitudes about money. Are there any cultural or regional differences in attitudes that you will face in this Money Talk? Is the immigrant experience "fresher" for some participants of the Money Talk than others?

2.10: Couple politics can also impact Money Talks, particularly when one partner surpasses the other in education and/or earning power. Are there any such issues that you will face in this Money Talk?

STEP 3: Plan the Money Talk physically, logistically and psychologically.

3.1: Have you ever held a Money Talk before? If so, what happened?

3.2: What do you think made earlier Money Talks successes or failures?

____

____

____

3.3: What are your concerns, if any, about holding this particular Money Talk?

____

____

____

3.4: What are your objectives or goals for this Money Talk? What do you want to accomplish?

____

____

____

3.5: What are the specific financial issues and topics you'll need to address that were identified in Step 1?

____

____

____

3.6: Are there any potentially problematic family issues that are likely to arise? Are there factors related to control, trust, family health, gender, marriage politics, evolutionary patterns, instinctive behavior, family history, culture, age, attitude, etc.? (Refer back to Chapters 8 and 11 in *The M Word*.)

____

____

____

3.7: Is there anyone in the family with whom communication is frequently challenging? If so, who?

3.8: Is there anything you can do to overcome these factors and individual challenges?

3.9: Using professional communication techniques (discussed in Chapter 9 in *The M Word*), answer who, what, when, where, and how to have the talk before sitting down for the conversations. Create an agenda based on the issues at play and the players that need to be present. Chapter 4 in *The M Word* includes a sample agenda and more discussion around creating one tailored to your talk.

3.10: Well in advance of the Money Talk, send a summary agenda to everyone who will be party to the conversation so they can be prepared to discuss the topics and, if appropriate, address them in advance with their advisor(s). Speak to each participant before the meeting regarding the meeting objectives and their particular concerns, and make any necessary changes to the agenda to reflect additional issues raised. Inform participants that communication devices are not permitted during the talks. Make sure you have agendas printed and available at the Money Talk as well.

3.11: Based on the agenda, write a "script" for exactly what you want to say and how you want to say it, and then rehearse it.

____

____

____

3.12: Consider times and settings for the talk that can create a safe and comfortable environment. (Refer to Chapter 8 in *The M Word.*)

____

____

____

3.13: To enhance the chances for success, apologize for any role you may have played in creating family conflict. Develop appropriate language and tone to help facilitate caring and cooperation.

____

____

____

3.14: Plan a question-and-answer session and your responses to anticipated concerns and expressions of anger or resentment using inquiry, acknowledgment, advocacy, and problem-solving techniques. (Refer to Chapter 9 in *The M Word*.)

3.15: Plan to discuss changes you will need to make to your current lifestyle that could impact other family members.

3.16: Plan to discuss changes to your long-term financial planning that could impact other family members.

STEP 4: Determine what professional help you may need for the Money Talk.

4.1: Do you have an advisor(s) who can help you with your collective and individual tax, estate, and financial planning?

☐ Yes

☐ No

4.2 If you have an advisor(s), have you discussed with them your ideal outcome for the talk and the financial issues and topics that may need to be discussed? If you do not have advisors, what professionals do you think you need in order to create the right team?

- ☐ Accountant
- ☐ Attorney
- ☐ Financial advisor
- ☐ Mental health professional
- ☐ Other

4.3: If you do have a team and you want to replace one or more members, who are they? Why are you not satisfied with them? What traits would you look for in replacement members that the current members of your team lack?

____

____

____

4.4: Does your advisor(s) have the right combination of licenses, credentials, experience, and knowledge in the areas you need?

- ☐ Yes
- ☐ No

4.5: Do they have the necessary character and chemistry as well as the communication skills you are looking for?

- ☐ Yes
- ☐ No

4.6: Are you prepared to do all the work that needs to be done to find the right advisor or team of advisors?

- ☐ Yes
- ☐ No

4.7: If you are not prepared to conduct the search, is there another member of your family who can do it? Is there a member of your professional team who can refer you to qualified professionals and may be capable of doing the initial search for you?

4.8: What situations are facing your family that you need to address in interviewing advisor candidates?

4.9: Is there anything unique about your family that should be discussed with potential advisors? Is there a special expertise you might need in order to deal with current or future issues?

4.10: Do any of your existing advisors appear to have the ability to act as team quarterback? If not, do any of the advisors you are interviewing appear to have the ability to act as quarterback?

4.11: Can any member of your advisory team help you prepare for the Money Talk or perhaps even lead it?

____

____

____

STEP 5: Anticipate and plan for future Money Talks.

5.1: Was the Money Talk a success? If so, why? If not, why?

____

____

____

5.2: Have you created a process that is repeatable, and have you planned for the multiple conversations that are probably necessary for accomplishing your goals?

____

____

____

5.3: What issues related to this transition, either newly developed or raised in the most recent Money Talk, will you need to discuss or review in the near future?

____

____

____

5.4: What is the best method for regular periodic money discussions if in-person discussions are not available for everyone for future talks?

- ☐ Telephone calls
- ☐ Skype/FaceTime
- ☐ Email/Text—for transmitting information only
- ☐ Other

5.5: When and where will you hold your next Money Talk? Who will prepare the next agenda and take the leadership role in planning?

____

____

____

ANNUIT COEPTIS
$

3
E PLURIBUS
UNUM

RETIREMENT PLANNING

Having Money Talks About Saving and Investing for Life After Work

The question isn't at what age I want to retire,
it's at what income.

—George Foreman

Increased life expectancy is seldom viewed as a negative. But when coupled with uncertainty about the economy, inflation, world financial markets, and income, a longer lifespan *does* make retirement planning more difficult. And for many baby boomers, millennials, and their families, the Great Recession's impact on finances is still being felt and has amplified the difficulties.

Plans may need to be adjusted to include additional years in the workforce to generate earned income and years when Social Security payments are delayed.

Investing choices may also need to be adjusted to account for the potential need for greater growth. In light of these changes, paying for education or education loans, buying a home, or contributions to non-dependent children and parents must be reexamined. This "new normal" demands a rethinking of everything from lifestyle choices to risk aversion.

Note: Before you address the specific issue you are facing, make sure you have updated your personal financial inventory and records. You will need access to the most up-to-date information in order to complete this *M Word Journal*, which is designed around the following five steps:

1. Gather information about the transition point you are facing, and identify and prepare for the issues and topics that need to be discussed.
2. Consider the factors that are interfering with your family having the Money Talk and how to overcome them.
3. Plan the Money Talk physically, logistically, and psychologically.
4. Determine what professional help you may need for the Money Talk.
5. Create a process, repeat it, and anticipate and plan for future Money Talks.

In order to make the most of this journal, you will need to make some additional assumptions and estimations before you begin, perhaps with the help of your financial advisor. I have included some figures that you can change, such as a life expectancy of 90 and a 2 percent inflation rate, but you should tailor the following to your specific situation:

- Age at retirement
- Life expectancy
- Inflation rate
- Rate of return on investments
- Tax rate on different income sources in retirement

PLEASE NOTE: For an in-depth discussion of the Money Talk and other concepts, see *The M Word: The Money Talk Every Family Needs to Have about Wealth and Their Financial Future* (McGraw-Hill Education, 2013, updated 2016).

STEP 1: Gather information about the transition point you are facing, and identify and prepare for the issues and topics that need to be discussed.

1.1: Prepare a family balance sheet.

ASSETS	TOTAL
Bank accounts	
Brokerage accounts	
Securities	
IRAs/Profit sharing/401(k) plans	
Stock options/Restricted stock/Deferred compensation	
Pensions/Annuities	
Insurance (cash value)	
Real estate	
Autos	
Home furnishings	
Collectibles	
Other/Business interests/etc.	
Total	

LIABILITIES	TOTAL
Mortgage balances	
Auto loans	
Personal loans	
Personal lines of credit	
Credit card balances	
Personally guaranteed business loans	
Other itemized debts	
Total	

Net worth[1]	

1.2: Review your family's current expenses and obligations, and estimate what those expenses and obligations will be in retirement.

EXPENSE	CURRENT MONTHLY	CURRENT ANNUALLY	ESTIMATED IN RETIREMENT
Primary home[2]			
Secondary home[3]			
Food			
Clothing			
Personal entertainment			
Utilities[4]			
Personal transportation[5]			
Debt service[6]			
Taxes			
Professional fees			

[1] Total assets minus total liabilities

[2] Include all expenses involved in the upkeep and maintenance of the property as well as any mortgage or rent payments.

[3] Include all expenses involved in the upkeep and maintenance of the property as well as any mortgage or rent payments.

[4] Include cell phone, pay television, and Internet services.

[5] Include any mass transit/commuting costs as well as auto lease or loan payments, auto insurance, fuel, repairs, and maintenance.

[6] Do NOT include home mortgages or children's student loans.

Travel			
Dues and memberships			
Insurance[7]			
Education[8]			
Child support			
Alimony			
Pension contribution			
Regular savings			
Total			

CONTRIBUTIONS TO ADULT, NON-DEPENDENT CHILDREN AND, PARENTS[9]	MONTHLY	ANNUALLY	ESTIMATED IN RETIREMENT
Total			

[7] Include medical as well as life, disability, homeowners, and umbrella/liability policies.

[8] Include tuition, room and board, books, and other education-related items.

[9] Itemize expenses.

1.3: Estimate your projected retirement income.

WHAT IS YOUR TOTAL INCOME?	MONTHLY	ANNUALLY
Earned income		
Investments/securities		
Business interests/ real estate		
Social Security and retirement assets		
Other sources		
Total		

1.4: Calculate the projected surplus or shortfall.

	MONTHLY	ANNUALLY
Total income in retirement		
Total retirement expenses, obligations		
Surplus or shortfall		

1.5: Estimate your life expectancies, your retirement ages, and the number of years of retirement income you and your spouse will need.

	SELF	SPOUSE
Life Expectancy	90	90
Estimate retirement age		
Estimated years of retirement		

NOTE: Speak with your financial advisor and accountant for help in calculating the next three tables.

1.6: Estimate an average rate of return from investments using your current assets and asset allocation, adjusted for inflation, both before and after retirement.

Estimated average rate of return from investments	
Minus estimated average rate of inflation	2%
Estimated average real rate of return	

1.7: Estimate your taxes in retirement based on your sources of income and its impact on your earned and unearned income.

Estimated annual earned income during retirement	
Estimated annual income from retirement assets	
Estimated annual income from nonretirement assets	
Less: estimated taxes during retirement from all sources	
Total estimated after tax income during retirement	

1.8: Using commercial financial-planning software or the planning services of your financial advisor:

- Calculate the assets you will need to be able to achieve your current lifestyle goals, based on life expectancies, estimated retirement expenses, and estimated income from all sources adjusted for inflation and taxes.
- Estimate the assets you will have at retirement, based on the number of years until retirement, additional annual savings before retirement, and average rate of return on investments.

How do they compare?

If you "have enough" based on assumptions, have you considered gifting, philanthropy, or asset-transfer strategies to minimize taxes and fulfill your legacy goals?

If your assumptions for current income, retirement expenses, assets available, investment strategies, and time horizons will not allow you to achieve your retirement lifestyle goals, you will need to consider changes to those strategies and goals.

1.9: Can you restructure/pay off any of your debts?

DEBT	MONTHLY SAVINGS	ANNUAL SAVINGS
Total		

1.10: Can you trim any of your own expenses and obligations?

EXPENSE	MONTHLY SAVINGS	ANNUAL SAVINGS
Total		

1.11: Can your family develop any new streams of income, such as a nonworking spouse going to work or a dependent child getting part-time employment?

ADDITIONAL STREAM OF INCOME	MONTHLY INCREASE	ANNUAL INCREASE
Total		

1.12: Consider reductions in support/gifts to adult non-dependent children, parents, and charitable donations.

SUPPORT/GIFT/CHARITY	MONTHLY SAVINGS	ANNUAL SAVINGS
Total		

1.13: Are you and/or your partner willing to extend your working lives and postpone retirement? If so, how long would you be willing to wait?

______

______

______

1.14: Are you and/or your spouse willing to work part time during retirement? If so, how much income could this yield and for how long?

______

______

______

1.15: Are you willing to assume greater investment risk and/or change your asset-allocation formula in order to increase your assets and create more potential growth and income?

______

______

______

STEP 2: Consider the factors that are interfering with your family having the Money Talk and how to overcome them.

2.1: How has money been used as a means of control in your immediate family? How has that affected the various relationships, and how does it continue to inform them?

2.2: In what ways are money and trust bound together in your immediate family culture? How does that play out in family relationships, collectively and individually?

2.3: What is the historical role of each member of the immediate family when it comes to money? Has someone been the caretaker while someone else always needed to be cared for? Has a member of the family always been responsible and independent, whereas another member has always been irresponsible and more dependent? And how will changes in the family and money structure affect these roles?

2.4: Accept that gender differences have roots in physiology and as a result, some conflicts are likely. Which differences will be at work in your situation: risk-taking, prioritizing of goals, setting a time horizon, or all three?

2.5: Be aware of the ingrained thinking patterns that influence decisions. What are the issues in this situation that could lead to a struggle between emotions and reason when it comes to making money decisions?

2.6: Understand that people are hardwired to see money as an object of threat and control and often respond instinctively. Which of the six basic instincts—shelter seeking, care soliciting, caregiving, cooperation, beauty, and curiosity—are likely to arise in each of the participants, and what are the best ways to address them? (Refer to Chapter 8 of *The M Word.)*

2.7: Understand generational differences in money perceptions and values. What generational differences will you face in this situation? What language can you use that is age- and generation-appropriate?

2.8: Think about your extended family's history with money. Has the relationship that your parents and grandparents had with money been passed down to any of the other participants in the Money Talk? For example, historically, has money been used as a substitute for love or a tool for control or for some other tactic? How might this history play out in the current situation, and how can you address it?

2.9: Understand that culture and experience affect attitudes about money. Are there any cultural or regional differences in attitudes that you will face in this Money Talk? Is the immigrant experience "fresher" for some participants of the Money Talk than others?

2.10: Couple politics can also impact Money Talks, particularly when one partner surpasses the other in education and/or earning power. Are there any such issues that you will face in this Money Talk?

STEP 3: Plan the Money Talk physically, logistically, and psychologically.

3.1: Have you ever held a Money Talk before? If so, what happened?

3.2: What do you think made earlier Money Talks successes or failures?

3.3: What are your concerns, if any, about holding this particular Money Talk?

____

____

____

3.4: What are your objectives or goals for this Money Talk? What do you want to accomplish?

____

____

____

3.5: What are the specific financial issues and topics you'll need to address that were identified in Step 1?

____

____

____

3.6: Are there any potentially problematic family issues that are likely to arise? Are there factors related to control, trust, family health, gender, marriage politics, evolutionary patterns, instinctive behavior, family history, culture, age, attitude, etc.? (Refer back to Chapters 8 and 11 in *The M Word*.)

____

____

____

3.7: Is there anyone in the family with whom communication is frequently challenging? If so, who?

____

____

____

3.8: Is there anything you can do to overcome these factors and individual challenges?

____

____

____

3.9: Using professional communication techniques (discussed in Chapter 9 in *The M Word*), answer who, what, when, where, and how to have the talk before sitting down for the conversations. Create an agenda based on the issues at play and the players that need to be present. Chapter 5 in *The M Word* includes a sample agenda and more discussion around creating one tailored to your talk.

____

____

____

3.10: Well in advance of the Money Talk, send a summary agenda to everyone who will be party to the conversation so they can be prepared to discuss the topics and, if appropriate, address them in advance with their advisor(s). Speak to each participant before the meeting regarding the meeting objectives and their particular concerns, and make any necessary changes to the agenda to reflect additional issues raised. Inform participants that communication devices are not permitted during the talks. Make sure you have agendas printed and available at the Money Talk as well.

3.11: Based on the agenda, write a "script" for exactly what you want to say and how you want to say it, and then rehearse it.

____

____

____

3.12: Consider times and settings for the talk that can create a safe and comfortable environment. (Refer to Chapter 8 in *The M Word.*)

3.13: To enhance the chances for success, apologize for any role you may have played in creating family conflict. Develop appropriate language and tone to help facilitate caring and cooperation.

3.14: Plan a question-and-answer session and your responses to anticipated concerns and expressions of anger or resentment using inquiry, acknowledgment, advocacy, and problem-solving techniques. (Refer to Chapter 9 in *The M Word.*)

3.15: Plan to discuss changes you will need to make to your current lifestyle that could impact other family members.

3.16: Plan to discuss changes to your long-term financial planning that could impact other family members.

STEP 4: Determine what professional help you may need for the Money Talk.

4.1: Do you have an advisor(s) who can help you with your taxes, estate planning, and financial plan?

- [ ] Yes
- [ ] No

4.2: If you have an advisor(s), have you discussed with them your ideal outcome for the talk and the financial issues and topics that may need to be discussed? If you do not have advisors, what professionals do you think you need in order to create the right team?

- [ ] Accountant
- [ ] Attorney
- [ ] Financial advisor
- [ ] Mental health professional
- [ ] Other

4.3: If you do have a team and you want to replace one or more members, who are they? Why are you not satisfied with them? What traits would you look for in replacement members that the current members of your team lack?

____

____

____

4.4: Does your advisor(s) have the right combination of licenses, credentials, experience, and knowledge in the areas you need?

- [ ] Yes
- [ ] No

4.5: Do they have the necessary character and chemistry as well as the communication skills you are looking for?

☐ Yes

☐ No

4.6: Are you prepared to do all the work that needs to be done to find the right advisor or team of advisors?

☐ Yes

☐ No

4.7: If you are not prepared to conduct the search, is there another member of your family who can do it? Is there a member of your professional team who can refer you to qualified professionals and may be capable of doing the initial search for you?

____

____

____

4.8: What situations are facing your family that you need to address in interviewing advisor candidates?

____

____

____

4.9: Is there anything unique about your family that should be discussed with potential team members? Is there a special expertise you might need in order to deal with current or future issues?

____

____

____

4.10: Do any of your existing advisors appear to have the ability to act as team quarterback? If not, do any of the advisors you are interviewing appear to have the ability to act as quarterback?

4.11: Can any member of your advisory team help you prepare for the Money Talk or perhaps even lead it?

STEP 5: Anticipate and plan for future Money Talks.

5.1: Was the Money Talk a success? If so, why? If not, why?

5.2: Have you created a process that is repeatable, and have you planned for multiple conversations probably necessary for accomplishing your goals?

5.3: What issues related to this transition, either newly developed or raised in the most recent Money Talk, will you need to discuss or review in the near future?

5.4: What is the best method for regular periodic money discussions if in-person discussions are not available for everyone for future talks?

- ☐ Telephone calls
- ☐ Skype/FaceTime
- ☐ Email/Text—for transmitting information only
- ☐ Other

5.5: When and where will you hold your next Money Talk? Who will prepare the next agenda and take the leadership role in planning?

E PLURIBUS
UNUM
$

4

CARING FOR AN ELDERLY PARENT

Having Money Talks about Parents' Long-Term Care

A test of a people is how it behaves toward the old. It is easy to love children. Even tyrants and dictators make a point of being fond of children. But the affection and care of the old, the incurable, the helpless are the true gold mines of a culture.

—Abraham J. Heschel

Increased longevity means the elderly population will continue to grow. The need for some form of elder care will grow as well. It's expected that 15 million older Americans will need long-term care by 2020. Most aging Americans are cared for at home, with family and friends serving as the sole caregivers for 70 percent of the elderly. But anyone reaching 65 has a 40 percent chance of entering a nursing home and a 20 percent chance of staying there for five years or more.

Wherever the care takes place, the cost is high and increasing: One out of six people who reach 65 will spend more than $100,000 annually on long-term care. With only about 9 percent of Americans having any form of private long-term-care insurance, this is a potential financial burden that needs to be planned for.

The physical, emotional, and mental strain on caregivers is no less daunting and just as vital to address. While one adult child typically steps forward to take on the responsibility of at least supervising elder care, it's essential that all family members get involved in one way or another and that outside experts be brought in to provide informed guidance. Caring for an elderly parent is not a do-it-yourself process.

Note: Before you address the specific issue you are facing, make sure you have updated your personal financial inventory and records. You will need access to the most up-to-date information in order to complete this *M Word Journal*, which is designed around the following five steps:

1. Gather information about the transition point you are facing, and identify and prepare for the issues and topics that need to be discussed.
2. Consider the factors that are interfering with your family having the Money Talk and how to overcome them.
3. Plan the Money Talk physically, logistically, and psychologically.
4. Determine what professional help you may need for the Money Talk.
5. Create a process, repeat it, and anticipate and plan for future Money Talks.

Please note: For an in-depth discussion of the Money Talk and other concepts, see *The M Word: The Money Talk Every Family Needs to Have about Wealth and Their Financial Future* (McGraw-Hill Education, 2013, updated 2016).

STEP 1: Gather information about the transition point you are facing, and identify and prepare for the issues and topics that need to be discussed.

1.1: Review your loved one's assets.

ASSET	AMOUNT
Bank accounts	
Brokerage accounts	
Securities	
IRAs/Profit sharing/401(K) plans	
Stock options/Restricted stock/Deferred compensation	
Pensions/Annuities	
Insurance (cash value)	
Real estate	
Autos	
Home furnishings	
Collectibles	
Other/Business interests/etc.	
Total	

1.2: Review your loved one's liabilities.

LIABILITY	AMOUNT
Mortgage balances	
Auto loans	
Personal loans	
Personal lines of credit	

1.2: Review your loved one's liabilities (continued).

LIABILITY	AMOUNT
Credit card balances	
Personally guaranteed business loans	
Other itemized debts	
Total	

1.3: Review your loved one's expenses.

EXPENSE	MONTHLY	ANNUALLY
Primary home[1]		
Secondary home[2]		
Care facility[3]		
Home care[4]		
Medical[5]		
Food		
Clothing		
Personal entertainment		
Utilities[6]		
Debt service[7]		
Personal transportation[8]		
Taxes		
Professional fees		
Dues and memberships		
Insurance[9]		
Regular cash gifts		
Total		

[1] Include all expenses involved in the upkeep and maintenance of the property as well as any mortgage or rent payments.

[2] Include all expenses involved in the upkeep and maintenance of the property as well as any mortgage or rent payments.

[3] Include all costs of care facility.

[4] Include all home care costs.

[5] Include out-of-pocket payments and copayments.

[6] Include cell phone, pay television, and Internet services.

[7] Do NOT include home mortgages.

[8] Include any mass transit/commuting costs as well as auto lease or loan payments, auto insurance, fuel, repairs, and maintenance.

[9] Include medical as well as life, disability, homeowners, and umbrella/liability policies.

1.4: Calculate your loved one's income.

WHAT IS YOUR LOVED ONE'S TOTAL INCOME?	MONTHLY	ANNUALLY
Earned income		
Investments/securities		
Business interests/ real estate		
Social Security and retirement assets		
Other sources		
Total		

1.5: Calculate your loved one's surplus or shortfall.

	MONTHLY	ANNUALLY
Total income		
Total expenses/obligations		
Surplus or shortfall		

1.6 After speaking with health care professionals, determine what your loved one's life expectancy may be.

1.7: If your loved one's income and future-income needs, based on her (or his) sources of income, assets available, and life expectancy, exceed what is required to care for her, have you considered ways to restructure her estate plan and gift and transfer assets? Have you met with her advisor(s) to discuss the matter?

1.8 If your loved one's expenses exceed income, can any of the expenses be reduced?

EXPENSE	MONTHLY SAVINGS	ANNUAL SAVINGS
Total		

1.9: Can you or other family members supplement your loved one's income?

FAMILY MEMBER	MONTHLY CONTRIBUTION	ANNUAL CONTRIBUTION
Total		

1.10: Can you or other family members provide additional caregiving time, reducing the cost of at-home care?

FAMILY MEMBER	HOURS OF ADDED AT-HOME CARE
Total	

1.11: Can any assets, such as a home, be sold to cover the additional expenses?

ASSET	DOLLARS UPON SALE

1.12: How much additional expense coverage can be generated by asset sales, expense reductions, and family contributions of money and time?

	TOTAL AMOUNT ($)	ADDITIONAL $ PER YR	# OF YRS
Asset sales			
Expense reductions			
Family contributions			
Total			

1.13: Consider the impact of rising costs of care on current monthly and annual expenses determined in Step 1.3. Will there be additional sources of income or reduction in expenses to cover rising care costs?

1.14: Has your loved one recently updated their estate plan to reflect their current circumstances and executed the following documents?

- ☐ Wills & Trusts
- ☐ Power of attorney with durable power of attorney clause included
- ☐ Health care proxy
- ☐ Living will
- ☐ HIPAA release
- ☐ DNR
- ☐ Other

STEP 2: **Consider the factors that are interfering with your family having the Money Talk and how to overcome them.**

2.1: How has money been used as a means of control in your immediate family? How has that affected the various relationships, and how does it continue to inform them?

2.2: In what ways are money and trust bound together in your immediate family culture? How does that play out in family relationships, collectively and individually?

2.3: What is the historical role of each member of the immediate family when it comes to money? Has someone been the caretaker while someone else always needed to be cared for? Has a member of the family always been responsible and independent, whereas another member has always been irresponsible and more dependent? And how will changes in the family and money structure affect these roles?

2.4: Accept that gender differences have roots in physiology and as a result, some conflicts are likely. Which differences will be at work in your situation: risk-taking, prioritizing of goals, setting a time horizon, or all three?

2.5: Be aware of the ingrained thinking patterns that influence decisions. What are the issues in this situation that could lead to a struggle between emotion and reason when it comes to making money decisions?

2.6: Understand that people are hardwired to see money as an object of threat and control and often respond instinctively. Which of the six basic instincts—shelter seeking, care soliciting, caregiving, cooperation, beauty, and curiosity—are likely to arise in each of the participants, and what are the best ways to address them? (Refer to Chapter 8 of *The M Word*.)

2.7: Understand generational differences in money perceptions and values. What generational differences will you face in this situation? What language can you use that's age- and generation-appropriate?

2.8: Think about your extended family's history with money. Has the relationship that parents and grandparents had with money been passed down to any of the other participants in the Money Talk? For example, historically, has money been used as a substitute for love or a tool for control or for some other tactic? How might this history play out in the current situation, and how can you address it?

2.9: Understand that culture and experience affect attitudes about money. Are there any cultural or regional differences in attitudes that you will face in this Money Talk? Is the immigrant experience "fresher" for some participants of the Money Talk than others?

2.10: Couple politics can also impact Money Talks, particularly when one partner surpasses the other in education and/or earning power. Are there any such issues that you will face in this Money Talk?

STEP 3: Plan the Money Talk physically, logistically, and psychologically.

3.1: Have you ever held a Money Talk before? If so, what happened?

3.2: What do you think made earlier Money Talks successes or failures?

3.3: What are your concerns, if any, about holding this particular Money Talk?

3.4: What are your objectives or goals for this Money Talk? What do you want to accomplish?

3.5: What are the specific financial issues and topics you'll need to address that were identified in Step 1?

3.6: Are there any potentially problematic family issues that are likely to arise? Are there factors related to control, trust, family health, gender, marriage politics, evolutionary patterns, instinctive behavior, family history, culture, age, attitude, etc.? (Refer back to Chapters 8 and 11 in *The M Word*.)

3.7: Is there anyone in the family with whom communication is frequently challenging? If so, who?

3.8: Is there anything you can do to overcome these factors and individual challenges?

3.9: Using professional communication techniques (discussed in Chapter 9 in *The M Word*), answer who, what, when, where, and how to have the talk before sitting down for the conversations. Create an agenda based on the issues at play and the players that need to be present. Chapter 6 in *The M Word* includes a sample agenda and more discussion around creating one tailored to your talk.

3.10: Well in advance of the Money Talk, send a summary agenda to everyone who will be party to the conversation so they can be prepared to discuss the topics and, if appropriate, address them in advance with their advisor(s). Speak to each participant before the meeting regarding the meeting objectives and their particular concerns, and make any necessary changes to the agenda to reflect additional issues raised. Inform participants that communication devices are not permitted during the talks. Make sure you have agendas printed and available at the Money Talk as well.

3.11: Based on the agenda, write a "script" for exactly what you want to say and how you want to say it, and then rehearse it.

3.12: Consider times and settings for the talk that can create a safe and comfortable environment. (Refer to Chapter 8 in *The M Word.*)

3.13: To enhance the chances for success, apologize for any role you may have played in creating family conflict. Develop appropriate language and the right tone to help foster caring and cooperation.

3.14: Plan a question-and-answer session and your responses to anticipated concerns and expressions of anger or resentment using inquiry, acknowledgment, advocacy, and problem solving techniques. (Refer to Chapter 9 in *The M Word.*)

3.15: Plan to discuss changes you will need to make to your current lifestyle that could impact other family members.

3.16: Plan to discuss changes to your long-term financial planning that could impact other family members.

STEP 4: Determine what professional help you may need for the Money Talk.

4.1: Do you have an advisor(s) who can help you with your collective and individual tax, estate, and financial planning?

- ☐ Yes
- ☐ No

4.2: If you have an advisor(s), have you discussed with them your ideal outcome for the talk and the financial issues and topics that may need to be discussed? If you do not have advisors, what professionals do you think you need in order to create the right team?

- ☐ Accountant
- ☐ Attorney
- ☐ Financial advisor
- ☐ Mental health professional
- ☐ Other

4.3: If you do have a team and you want to replace one or more members, who are they? Why are you not satisfied with them? What traits would you look for in replacement members that the current members of your team lack?

___

___

___

4.4: Does your advisor(s) have the right combination of licenses, credentials, experience, and knowledge in the areas you need?

- ☐ Yes
- ☐ No

4.5: Do they have the necessary character and chemistry as well as the communication skills you are looking for?

- ☐ Yes
- ☐ No

4.6: Are you prepared to do all the work that needs to be done to find the right advisor or team of advisors?

- ☐ Yes
- ☐ No

4.7: If you are not prepared to conduct the search, is there another member of your family who can do it? Is there a member of your professional team who can refer you to qualified professionals and may be capable of doing the initial search for you?

____

____

____

4.8: What situations are facing your family that you need to address in interviewing advisor candidates?

____

____

____

4.9: Is there anything unique about your family that should be discussed with potential advisors? Is there a special expertise you might need in order to deal with current or future issues?

____

____

____

4.10: Do any of your existing advisors appear to have the ability to act as team quarterback? If not, do any of the advisors you are interviewing appear to have the ability to act as quarterback?

____

____

____

4.11: Can any member of your advisory team help you prepare for the Money Talk or perhaps even lead it?

____

____

____

STEP 5: Anticipate and plan for future Money Talks.

5.1: Was the Money Talk a success? If so, why? If not, why?

____

____

____

5.2: Have you created a process that is repeatable and have you planned for multiple conversations probably necessary for accomplishing your goals?

____

____

____

5.3: What issues related to this transition, either newly developed or raised in the most recent Money Talk, will you need to discuss or review in the near future?

5.4: What is the best method for regular periodic money discussions if in-person discussions are not available for everyone for future talks?

- ☐ Telephone calls
- ☐ Skype/FaceTime
- ☐ Emails/Text—for transmitting information only
- ☐ Other

5.5: When and where will you hold your next Money Talk? Who will prepare the next agenda and take the leadership role in planning?

5
NOVUS ORDO SECLORUM
MDCCLXXVI

PREPARING HEIRS AND ESTATE TRANSFERS

Having Money Talks about Intergenerational Family Wealth

Another good thing about being poor is that when you are seventy your children will not have declared you legally insane in order to gain control of your estate.

—Woody Allen

There has never been a more compelling need to have in-depth conversations about family wealth and to educate family members about the critically important subject of preparing heirs and estate transfers. That's because there is a 70 percent failure rate worldwide when it comes to transferring wealth from one generation to another, according to studies by the Massachusetts Institute of Technology, *The Economist*, and Roy Williams and Vic Preisser, authors of *Preparing Heirs: Five Steps to a Successful Transition of Family Wealth and Values*. And, according to the Center on Wealth and Philanthropy at Boston College, a huge amount of wealth is currently being passed along. An estimated $15 trillion will be transferred between 2007 and 2026 and more than $59 trillion between 2007 and 2061.

What are the primary causes of most of the failed wealth transfers? The main reason is one that everyone has experience with: a breakdown in communication and trust. Of course, it's understandable to want to avoid issues that relate to death, but ignoring or avoiding these issues just postpones and prolongs anxiety. Avoidance can also result in huge losses and costly mistakes. Finally, by preparing your heirs, you give them a chance to do their own better-informed financial planning.

Note: Before you address the specific issue you are facing, make sure you have updated your personal financial inventory and records. You will need access to the most up-to-date information in order to complete this M Word Journal, which is designed around the following five steps:

1. Gather information about the transition point you are facing, and identify and prepare for the issues and topics that need to be discussed.
2. Consider the factors that are interfering with your family having the Money Talk and how to overcome them.
3. Plan the Money Talk physically, logistically, and psychologically.
4. Determine what professional help you may need for the Money Talk.
5. Create a process, repeat it, and anticipate and plan for future Money Talks.

Please note: For an in-depth discussion of the Money Talk and other concepts, see *The M Word: The Money Talk Every Family Needs to Have about Wealth and Their Financial Future* (McGraw-Hill Education, 2013, updated 2016).

STEP 1: Gather information about the transition point you are facing, and identify and prepare for the issues and topics that need to be discussed.

1.1: Prepare a family balance sheet.

ASSETS	TOTAL
Bank accounts	
Brokerage accounts	
Securities	
IRAs/Profit sharing/401(k) plans	
Stock options/Restricted stock/Deferred compensation	
Pensions/Annuities	
Insurance (cash value)	
Real estate	
Autos	
Home furnishings	
Collectibles	
Other/Business interests/etc.	
Total	

LIABILITIES	TOTAL
Mortgage balances	
Auto loans	
Personal loans	
Personal lines of credit	
Personally guaranteed business loans	
Unpaid taxes and interest	
Other itemized debts	
Total liabilities	

Net worth[1]	

[1] Total assets minus total liabilities

1.2: Prepare a list of noteworthy personal property.

DESCRIPTION	$ VALUE	♥ VALUE[2]	RECIPIENT[3]

[2] Characterize the emotional value of the object as high, moderate, or low.

[3] Note if the item has already been given or promised to a particular heir. Otherwise, fill in the column during and after the Money Talk.

1.3: Prepare a list of previous, ongoing, and planned future financial contributions to heirs.

RECIPIENT[4]	TOTAL ANNUAL GIFTS[5]	TOTAL LUMP SUM GIFTS[6]	TOTAL OF GIFTS YTD	TOTAL PLANNED FUTURE GIFTS

1.4: Have you evaluated your resources and will you have enough to sustain your lifestyle needs for your family's life expectancies? Have you done the exercises and calculations in *The M Word Journal* "Retirement Planning" chapter?

1.5: Are there any other issues that you have identified requiring special attention?

____

____

____

1.6: If one of your heirs has special needs that will require special treatment after your demise, have you discussed this issue with your other heirs? Discuss the following options for providing for these needs with your financial advisor:

- ☐ Special needs trust
- ☐ Insurance policies
- ☐ Specific percentage or designated asset of estate

[4] Identify children, grandchildren, and others.

[5] Annual amount multiplied by number of years given

[6] If it was a loan, make note of the terms.

1.7: If you have sufficient assets for your family's life expectancies and the additional vehicles make sense, consider establishing one or more formal structures that will encourage family financial involvement, provide educational opportunities, and potentially offer financial benefits. Discuss the following options with your financial and legal advisors:

- ☐ Family foundation
- ☐ Involvement in a specific charitable organization
- ☐ Family limited partnership or Limited Liability Corporation
- ☐ Family Trust
- ☐ Other

1.8: Discuss different trust options with your financial and legal advisors, including Generation Skipping Transfer and insurance trusts, and take into account differences in how many children each heir has.

1.9: Ask your financial advisor and/or attorney to prepare simple outlines of your estate plan based on the ages and levels of comprehension of your heirs.

1.10: Distribute simple outlines of your plans to your heirs in advance of the Money Talk so they can review them with their own advisors, if appropriate.

STEP 2: Consider the factors that are interfering with your family having the Money Talk and how to overcome them.

2.1: How has money been used as a means of control in your immediate family? How has that affected the various relationships, and how does it continue to inform them?

2.2: In what ways are money and trust bound together in your immediate family culture? How does that play out in family relationships, collectively and individually?

2.3: What is the historical role of each member of the immediate family when it comes to money? Has someone been the caretaker while someone else always needed to be cared for? Has a member of the family always been responsible and independent, whereas another member has always been irresponsible and more dependent? And how will changes in the family and money structure affect these roles?

2.4: Accept that gender differences have roots in physiology and as a result, some conflicts are likely. Which differences will be at work in your situation: risk-taking, prioritizing of goals, setting a time horizon, or all three?

2.5: Be aware of the ingrained thinking patterns that influence decisions. What are the issues in this situation that could lead to a struggle between emotion and reason when it comes to making money decisions?

2.6: Understand that people are hardwired to see money as an object of threat and control and often respond instinctively. Which of the six basic instincts—shelter seeking, care soliciting, caregiving, cooperation, beauty, and curiosity—are likely to arise in each of the participants, and what are the best ways to address them?

2.7: Understand generational differences in money perceptions and values. What generational differences will you face in this situation? What language can you use that's age- and generation-appropriate?

2.8: Think about your extended family's history with money. Has the relationship that parents and grandparents had with money been passed down to any of the other participants in the Money Talk? For example, historically, has money been used as a substitute for love or a tool for control or for some other tactic? How might this history play out in the current situation, and how can you address it?

2.9: Understand that culture and experience affect attitudes about money. Are there any cultural or regional differences in attitudes that you will face in this Money Talk? Is the immigrant experience "fresher" for some participants of the Money Talk than others?

____

____

____

2.10: Couple politics can also impact Money Talks, particularly when one partner surpasses the other in education and/or earning power. Are there any such issues that you will face in this Money Talk?

____

____

____

STEP 3: Plan the Money Talk physically, logistically, and psychologically.

3.1: Have you ever held a Money Talk before? If so, what happened?

____

____

____

3.2: What do you think made earlier Money Talks successes or failures?

____

____

____

3.3: What are your concerns, if any, about holding this particular Money Talk?

3.4: What are your objectives or goals for this Money Talk? What do you want to accomplish?

3.5: What are the specific financial issues and topics you'll need to address that were identified in Step 1?

3.6: Are there any potentially problematic family issues that are likely to arise? Are there factors related to control, trust, family health, gender, marriage politics, evolutionary patterns, instinctive behavior, family history, culture, age, attitude, etc.? (Refer back to Chapters 8 and 11 in *The M Word*.)

3.7: Is there anyone in the family with whom communication is frequently challenging? If so, who?

3.8: Is there anything you can do to overcome these factors and individual challenges?

____

____

____

3.9: Using professional communication techniques (discussed in Chapter 9 in *The M Word*), answer who, what, when, where, and how to have the talk before sitting down for the conversations. Create an agenda based on the issues at play and the players that need to be present. Chapter 7 in *The M Word* includes a sample agenda and more discussion around creating one tailored to your talk.

____

____

____

3.10: Well in advance of the Money Talk, send a summary agenda to everyone who will be party to the conversation so they can be prepared to discuss the topics, and, if appropriate, address them in advance with their advisor(s). Speak to each participant before the meeting regarding the meeting objectives and their particular concerns, and make any necessary changes to the agenda to reflect additional issues raised. Inform participants that communication devices are not permitted during the talks. Make sure you have agendas printed and available at the Money Talk as well.

3.11: Based on the agenda, write a "script" for exactly what you want to say and how you want to say it, and then rehearse it.

____

____

____

3.12: Consider times and settings for the talk that can create a safe and comfortable environment. (Refer to Chapter 8 in *The M Word.*)

____

____

____

3.13: To enhance the chances for success, apologize for any role you may have played in creating family conflict. Develop appropriate language and the right tone to help facilitate caring and cooperation.

____

____

____

3.14: Plan a question-and-answer session and your responses to anticipated concerns and expressions of anger or resentment using inquiry, acknowledgment, advocacy, and problem solving techniques. (Refer to Chapter 9 in *The M Word.*)

____

____

____

3.15: Plan to discuss changes you will need to make to your current lifestyle that could impact other family members.

____

____

____

3.16: Plan to discuss changes to your long-term financial planning that could impact other family members.

____

____

____

STEP 4: Determine what professional help you may need for the Money Talk.

4.1: Do you have an advisor(s) who can help you with your taxes, estate planning, and financial plan?

- ☐ Yes
- ☐ No

4.2 If you have an advisor(s), have you discussed with them your ideal outcome for the talk and the financial issues and topics that may need to be discussed? If you do not have advisors, what professionals do you think you need in order to create the right team?

- ☐ Attorney
- ☐ Financial advisor
- ☐ Accountant
- ☐ Mental health professional
- ☐ Other

4.3: If you do have a team and you want to replace one or more members, who are they? Why are you not satisfied with them? What traits would you look for in replacement members that the current members of your team lack?

____

____

____

4.4: Does your advisor(s) have the right combination of licenses, credentials, experience, and knowledge in the areas you need?

- ☐ Yes
- ☐ No

4.5: Do they have the necessary character and chemistry as well as the communication skills you are looking for?

☐ Yes

☐ No

4.6: Are you prepared to do all the work that needs to be done to find the right advisor or team of advisors?

☐ Yes

☐ No

4.7: If you are not prepared to conduct the search, is there another member of your family who can do it? Is there a member of your professional team who can refer you to qualified professionals and may be capable of doing the initial search for you?

____

____

____

4.8: What situations are facing your family that you need to address in interviewing advisor candidates?

____

____

____

4.9: Is there anything unique about your family that should be discussed with potential team members? Is there a special expertise you might need in order to deal with current or future issues?

____

____

____

4.10: Do any of your existing advisors appear to have the ability to act as team quarterback? If not, do any of the advisors you are interviewing appear to have the ability to act as quarterback?

____

____

____

4.11: Can any member of your advisory team help you prepare for the Money Talk or perhaps even lead it?

____

____

____

STEP 5: Anticipate and plan for future Money Talks.

5.1: Was the Money Talk a success? If so, why? If not, why?

____

____

____

5.2: Have you created a process that is repeatable, and have you planned for multiple conversations probably necessary for accomplishing your goals?

____

____

____

5.3: What issues related to this transition, either newly developed or raised in the most recent Money Talk, will you need to discuss or review in the near future?

5.4: What is the best method for regular periodic money discussions if in-person discussions are not available for everyone for future talks?

- ☐ Telephone calls
- ☐ Skype/FaceTime
- ☐ Emails/Text—for transmitting information only
- ☐ Other

5.5: When and where will you hold your next Money Talk? Who will prepare the next agenda and take the leadership role in planning?

$
NOVUS ORDO SECLORUM
MDCCLXXVI

CPSIA information can be obtained at www.ICGtesting.com
Printed in the USA
BVOW03*0902250516

448784BV00005B/2/P

9 781633 932586